Super Predator
BALD EAGLE

by TJ Rob

Super-Predators: BALD EAGLE
By TJ Rob

Copyright Text TJ Rob, 2017

All rights reserved. No part of the book may be reproduced in any form without permission in writing from the author. Reviewers may quote brief passages in review.

Disclaimer

No part of this book may be reproduced in any form or by any means, mechanical or electronic, including photocopying or recording, or by an information storage and retrieval system, or transmitted by email without permission in writing from the publisher. This book is for entertainment purposes only. The views expressed are those of author alone.

Published by:
TJ Rob
Suite 609
440-10816 Macleod Trail SE
Calgary, AB T2J 5N8 www.TJRob.com

ISBN 978-1-988695-59-4

Photo Credits: Images used under license from Flickr.com, Pixabay.com, Public Domain, Wikimedia Commons, PublicDomainPictures.net, Pixnio.com:

Cover page, Michelle Buntin / Pixnio.com; Back Page, Nigel / Flickr.com; pg. 1, Andy Morffew / Flickr.com; pg. 2, USFWS Midwest / Flikr.com; pg. 3, USFWS Midwest / Flikr.com; pg. 4, Andy Morffew / Flickr.com; pg. 5, DGriebeling / Flickr.com; pg. 6, Mad Max CC BY-SA 3.0 / Via Wikimeaida Commons; pg. 7, Mad Max CC BY-SA 3.0 / Via Wikimeaida Commons; pg. 8, Isaac Sanchez / Flickr.com; pg. 9, Angell Williams / Flickr.com; pg. 10, OpenClipart-Vectors / Pixabay.com; pg. 11, LindseyRoseHoule / Pixabay.com; pg. 12, pxhere.com; pg. 13, Ssolbergj CC BY-SA 3.0 / Wikimedia Commons; pg. 14, Andy Morffew / Flickr.com; pg. 15, the 3cats / Pixabay.com; pg. 15, Andy Morffew / Flickr.com; pg. 16, emmeffe6 / Flickr.com; pg. 16, USFWS Mountain-Prairie / Flickr.com; pg. 16, Connor Mah / Flickr.com; pg. 16, OpenClipart-Vectors / Pixabay.com; pg. 17, Yellowstone National Park / Flickr.com; pg. 18, Skeeze / Pixabay.com; pg. 19, WikiPedant CC BY-SA 4.0 / via Wikimedia Commons; pg. 20, Craig Lymm / Flickr.com; pg. 21, Jim Bauer / Flickr.com; pg. 22, the 3cats / Pixabay.com; pg. 23, USFWS Midwest / Flikr.com; pg. 24, Michelle Smith / Pixnio.com; pg. 25, Liam Quinn / Flickr.com; pg. 26, Klaus Rassinger & Gerhard Cammerer, Wiesbaden Museum, CC BY-SA 3.0 / via Wikimedia Commons; pg. 26, Ren West CC BY 2.0 / via Wikimedia Commons; pg. 27, David Menke - United States Fish and Wildlife Service / via Wikimedia Commons; pg. 28, Murray Foubister / Flickr.com; pg. 29, KetaDesign CC BY 3.0 / via Wikimedia Commons; pg. 30, Skeeze / Pixabay.com; pg. 31, Angell Williams / Flickr.com; pg. 32, tpsdave / Pixabay.com; pg. 33, Chiara Martinelli CC BY-SA 3.0 / via Wikimedia Commons; pg. 34, Nalin Kumara / Flickr.com; pg. 35, Nalin Kumara / Flickr.com; pg. 36, AWWE83 CC BY-SA 3.0 / via Wikimedia Commons; pg. 37, AWWE83 CC BY-SA 3.0 / via Wikimedia Commons

TABLE OF CONTENTS

	Page
What are Bald Eagles?	4
What do Bald Eagles look like?	5
Where do Bald Eagles Live?	6
Are Bald Eagles really bald?	8
How many Bald Eagles are left in the Wild?	9
How Big is a Bald Eagle?	10
How long do Bald Eagles live?	11
An American Symbol	12
Hunting	14
What do Bald Eagles like to Eat?	16
How much do Bald Eagles Eat?	17
Cool Bald Eagle Facts	18
Bald Eagles Super Sight	19
Bald Eagles Senses	20
The Bald Eagle Call	21
Feathers and Flying	22
Nest Building	24
Bald Eagle Babies	26
More Cool Bald Eagle Facts	30
Do Bald Eagles Migrate?	31
How and Where do Bald Eagles Sleep?	32
Aerial Acrobats	33
How have Bald Eagles Adapted to their Environment?	34
Threats	36
Please leave a review / OTHER books by TJ Rob	38

What are Bald Eagles?

Bald Eagles are large birds that hunt and kill other animals for food.

All Bald Eagles have a hooked beak, fantastic eyesight, sharp talons and strong legs and feet.

Bald Eagles are Raptors or Birds of Prey.

The word 'raptor' comes from the Latin word, "rapere", which means to hold, seize or capture - something that Bald Eagles are really good at, and that makes them great hunters.

What do Bald Eagles look like?

Adult Bald Eagles have dark brown feathers on their body and wings, and white feathers on their head and tail. The adult's beak and feet are yellow.

In their first year of life, young Bald Eagles have dark brown feathers over their body, wings, head and tail. Their beaks and eyes are also dark.

At 3 to 4 years of age they begin to develop the white head and tail of the adult. Their beak and eyes also lighten in color as they reach adulthood. When they are about 5 to 6 years old, Bald Eagles will have a completely white head and tail.

Yellow eyes

Yellow beak

White head

Dark brown body

Yellow feet

White tail

Where do Bald Eagles Live?

Green color indicates where Bald Eagles live.

6

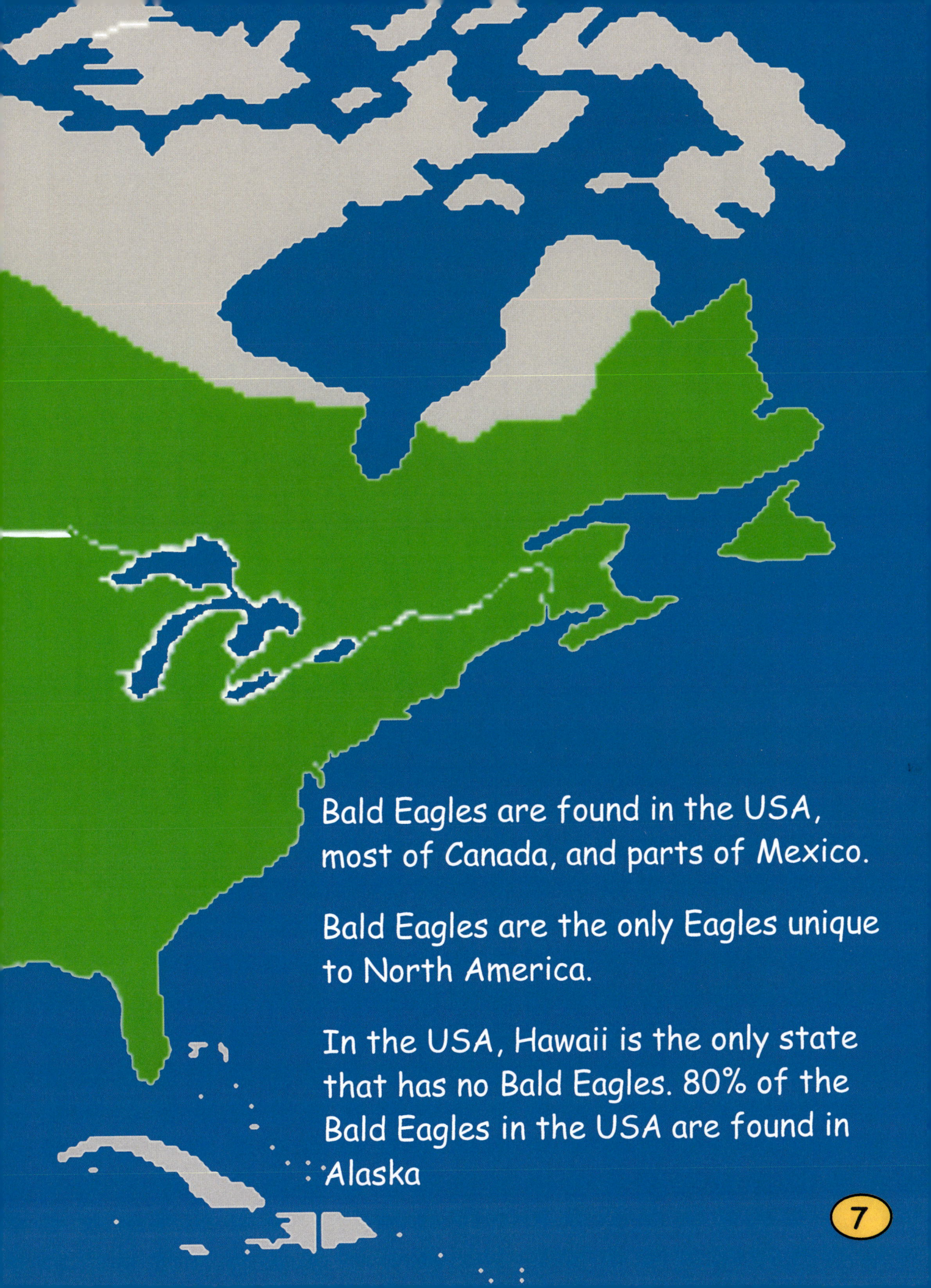

Bald Eagles are found in the USA, most of Canada, and parts of Mexico.

Bald Eagles are the only Eagles unique to North America.

In the USA, Hawaii is the only state that has no Bald Eagles. 80% of the Bald Eagles in the USA are found in Alaska

Are Bald Eagles really bald?

Bald Eagles are mainly brown with a white head and white tail feathers.

Why are they called Bald Eagles when they really have white feathers on their heads?

The name actually comes from an old English word — "piebald" — which meant "white headed" rather than hairless or bald.

How many Bald Eagles are left in the Wild?

Since the 1970's, the number of Bald Eagles has been steadily rising. Today Bald Eagles are no longer an Endangered Species.

1700's	200,000 - 400,000
1850's	Numbers dropping
1963	500 breeding pairs left, ENDANGERED
TODAY	70000 and RISING

How Big is a Bald Eagle?

Bald Eagles are big birds.

The Bald Eagle has a body length of 34 - 43 inches (86 – 109 cm). Wingspan is between 6 and 8 feet (1.83 and 2.44 m). Weight is between 6.6 and 14.5 pounds (3 and 6.5 kg).

Females are about 25% larger than males.

Bald Eagle size compared to a 6 foot (1.83 m) Man

The size of the bird varies by location. The further away from the Equator, the larger the average Bald Eagle size.

For example, Bald Eagles from South Carolina are smaller than Bald Eagles from Alaska. The largest Bald Eagles are from Alaska.

How long do Bald Eagles live?

A pair of Bald Eagles

The average life expectancy of Bald Eagles in the wild is between 20 and 30 years. The oldest confirmed wild Bald Eagle was 38 years old.

Bald Eagles in captivity live longer - some reaching life spans of 50 years.

An American Symbol

2 American Symbols: The Flag and the Bald Eagle

The Bald Eagle has been the National Bird and National Symbol of the USA for over 230 years.

The Bald Eagle was first chosen in 1782 and officially adopted as the emblem of the USA by Congress in 1789.

Eagles have been used as symbols of authority and power since Roman times. The Bald Eagle was thought to be chosen because of its great strength, good looks and long life. Also, it was believed that Bald Eagles could only be found in North America.

Today, the symbol of the Bald Eagle with outstretched wings can be found on gold coins, the silver dollar, the half dollar and the quarter in the USA.

The Bald Eagle can also be found on American passports, official State Documents, the US Coat Of Arms and the US President's Official Seal.

In 1969, the Lunar Module belonging to the Apollo 11 Space Mission (which landed on the Moon), was named "Eagle" after the American National Bird, the Bald Eagle.

The US Coat Of Arms features a Bald Eagle

Hunting

Bald Eagles are skilled hunters.

To catch fish, Bald Eagles watch the water surface from a perch, or while soaring in the air. Then they swoop down close to the water in a shallow glide and snatch the fish out of the water with a quick grab, using the very sharp and powerful talons (claws) on their feet.

Bald Eagles also steal food from other Bald Eagles and other birds of prey. Usually, chasing after another bird of prey is enough to encourage it to drop its catch, but sometimes a Bald Eagle will attack the other bird to steal its prey.

They also eat the decaying flesh of dead animals (carrion), like a deer hit by a car. Carrion is an important food source in the Winter when other foods are more difficult to find.

Catching a fish

Each Bald Eagle foot has 4 very sharp Talons. 3 in the front facing backwards and 1 larger talon in the back facing forward.

The leg muscles give the grip strength to the talons.

The crushing force of each talon is estimated to be at least 400 pounds per square inch (psi) per talon - enough to do plenty of damage to any prey.

3 front talons
1 back talon

Bald Eagles can kill prey many times their size, but they can only lift about one third of their body weight using their wings - just a few pounds.

If a Bald Eagle catches a fish that is too heavy to lift out of the water, the Bald Eagle does not let go of its prey.

It can "swim" a short distance on the surface of the water to the land. It drags the fish - still gripped in its talons - through the water, and uses its wings like the oars of a boat to paddle and "swim" to shore.

Having a swim

What do Bald Eagles like to Eat?

Bald Eagles love to eat fish, all kinds of fish.

Because fish is what they prefer to eat, Bald Eagles live along the coast, as well as by lakes and rivers.

Bald Eagles also eat a variety of other animals and birds. Their prey includes water birds like Ducks and Gulls, and small animals like Squirrels, Muskrats, Turtles, Prairie Dogs, Raccoons and Rabbits.

Salmon

Muskrat

Duck

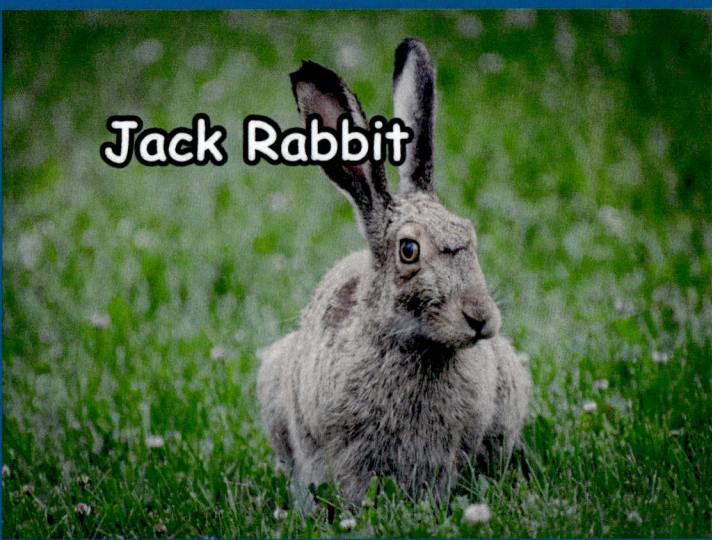

Jack Rabbit

How much do Bald Eagles Eat?

A Bald Eagle can eat 1 pound (.45 kg) of fish in about 4 minutes.

To eat, the Bald Eagle holds its prey with one foot, and anchors itself with the other foot. It then tears off each bite with its sharp, hooked beak.

Bald Eagles do not have to eat every day, but they cannot go without food for very long. If a bird goes too long without food, it may not have the strength to hunt well enough to survive.

Bald Eagles do have a secret weapon. They can store some of their food in a special pouch in their esophagus, called a crop. When their stomach is full, they store food in their crop to eat later.

Feeding time!

Cool Bald Eagle Facts:

1. Bald Eagles can dive at speeds of up to 100 miles per hour to snatch a fish from the water.

2. Bald Eagles were removed from the endangered species list in 2007.

3. Bald Eagles have hollow bones - their skeletons make up only 5 to 6% of their body weight.

4. Bald Eagles are considered to be sacred by many Native Americans. They are believed to be messengers of the Gods. Their feathers are used in ceremonial headdresses and costumes.

5. Bald Eagles are also known as American Eagles.

6. It is illegal to collect Bald Eagle feathers in the US. If you find a Bald Eagle feather on the ground in the US, you need a permit to pick it up.

7. Bald Eagles started to appear on coins in the US as early as 1776.

Bald Eagles Super Sight

Bald Eagles are famous for their excellent eyesight.

Bald Eagles can see both forward and to the side at the same time. Bald Eagles are able to see fish in the water from hundreds of feet in air. This is amazing because it is difficult to see fish from up close above the water, because most fish are darker on top.

Bald Eagles have eyelids that close during sleep. They also have an inner eyelid called a nictitating membrane. Every three or four seconds, the nictitating membrane slides across the eye, wiping dirt and dust from the surface of the eye. Because the membrane is clear, a Bald Eagle can see through it even while it is over the eye.

The yellow eye of an adult Bald Eagle

Even though a Bald Eagle weighs only 15 pounds (6.8 kg), it has the same size eye as a human weighing 200 pounds (91 kg).

Bald Eagles see the world in color, and they see colors more brightly than humans do too. A Bald Eagle's eyesight is 4 to 8 times better than that of a person with perfect vision. A Bald Eagle would be able to spot and identify a Rabbit moving almost 1 mile (1.6 km) away. Flying at a height of 1000 feet (300 m) over open country, it could spot prey over an area of almost 3 square miles (7.75 square km).

Bald Eagles Sense

HEARING
Though not as good as their eyesight, Bald Eagles do have excellent hearing.

Bald Eagles do not have large ears like we do. Their ears are small openings on both sides of the head behind the eyes. Their ears are covered with their head feathers, and are not visible unless you look for them.

SMELL
There are 2 nostrils at the top of the beak. Just like with humans, this is one way that Bald Eagles can breathe.

It is thought that like most birds, Bald Eagles do not have a good sense of smell. We do know that Bald Eagles do not use their sense of smell to find their prey.

Nostrils on both sides of the beak

The Bald Eagle Call

Because the Bald Eagle is a powerful bird of prey, you would expect its call to be loud and powerful.

The call of a Bald Eagle is surprisingly weak. People who have heard their call say that it sounds like a cackling laugh, or a group of high pitched whistling sounds.

Because the call of the Bald Eagle is not that impressive, Hollywood movies and TV shows often replace the actual call of the bald Eagle with the call of the Red-Tailed Hawk.

Bald Eagles do communicate using their calls. They call to each other to let other birds and predators know that this is their territory and it is defended. Some calls are a way to attract a mate. Bald Eagles also use chirping sounds to communicate with their young.

Feathers and Flying

Bald Eagles have 7,000 feathers. They molt (lose their feathers once a year) and replace their flight feathers with newer, stronger ones.

Feathers interlock with one another. The shafts of the feathers are hollow and this makes the feather very light but very strong. The layers of feathers trap air to insulate against cold and protect from the rain.

The primary, or main, feathers are rounded at the tips. They control lift and directional movement. The wings on airplanes are shaped similar to Eagles wings. This shape is great for lift off the ground. Tail feathers act as a rudder and help stabilize the bird during flight.

Interlocking feathers with rounded tips

Gliding up in the sky

Bald Eagles can fly to an altitude of 10,000 feet. During level flight, they can reach speeds of about 30 to 35 mph (50 to 56 km/h). Gliding speeds can reach 75 mph (120 km/h) and diving speeds up to 100 mph (160 km/h).

Bald Eagles can fly for 2 to 4 hours without landing.

Bald Eagle hunting areas vary from 1,700 to 10,000 acres (688 to 4,050 hectares).

To get off the ground, Bald Eagles flap their wings to reach altitude. Once they get to altitude, they glide and soar. They use updrafts and thermals (rising currents of warm air) to gain altitude so they can soar and glide even longer. The birds use much less energy by soaring and gliding than flapping their wings.

Nest Building

Bald Eagles are the World Champions in nest building.

Their nests often weigh 1,000 pounds (453 kg) or more. The biggest nest ever found was in St. Petersburg Florida in 1963. The nest measured 9.5 feet wide (2.9 meters) wide and 20 feet (6 meters) deep. It weighed more than 4,410 pounds (2,000 kg).

A giant nest!

Bald eagles choose a mate for life. Both male and female build the nest together. They start working on their nest 1 to 3 months before the female lays the first egg.

Both Eagles bring sticks to add to the nest structure. They interweave the sticks and fill in spaces with grasses, mosses and other fibers. To soften the bottom, parents line the nest with their own feathers.

Bald Eagles return to the same nest every year. Each year the adult pair will add 1 to 2 feet (0.3 to 0.6 m) of new material to the nest - that is how the nests become so big.

If a pair of Bald Eagles was successful at producing young at a nest, they are more likely to return to that nest again the next year. They might choose to build a new nest in a different area if they did not produce Eaglets at the previous nest.

Bald Eagles choose the tallest living tree close to water to build their nest, so that they can catch their favorite food - fish.

At the top of a tree!

When they build a new nest from scratch, nest building may take 1 to 3 months. Sometimes after using a nest year after year, the nest becomes too heavy for the tree. Then the Bald Eagle pair might build a nest in the same area, close to the previous nest.

Some Bald Eagles will have two nests. They may use one nest for a few years and then move to the second nest for another few years, giving the first nest time to air out. Bald Eagles will defend their nests from other Eagles and birds of prey.

Bald Eagle Babies

Mating season depends on the region where the birds live. The further South, the earlier the start of the mating season. In Southern areas like Florida, mating season may start in September through November. Eggs are laid in March and April. In Alaska and Northern Canada, mating season is from January through to March, with eggs being laid in May through June.

Bald Eagles start to mate when they reach 4 to 5 years old, the age when they have their adult colors - the white head and tail feathers, and brown body feathers.

The female lays 1 to 3 eggs, 2 being the most common number. The eggs take between 1 to 1 1/2 months (about 35 to 40 days) to hatch. Both the male and female will take a turn of sitting on the eggs, though the female does most of the sitting.

Bald Eagle Egg

Chicken Egg

Bald Eagle babies are called Eaglets. Eaglets are speckled brown and white in color. After hatching, Eaglets are wet, exhausted, and almost blind. Their eyes are dark brown in color and are closed at hatching. They open after a few hours.

Eaglets

For the first few weeks after hatching an Eaglet is not able to regulate its own body temperature and relies on the parents to keep it warm. On sunny days, parents sometimes spread their wings to make shade for their young.

After hatching both the male and female feed their young until they learn to fly. For the first 2 to 3 three weeks after hatching, at least one parent is in the nest almost 100% of the time, while the other parent looks for food and material to repair the nest.

Bald Eagle Babies

After 3 or 4 weeks the Eaglet's feathers begin to change color. Darker feathers begin to form on back, shoulder, breast and wings, and flight feathers start to develop.

From day 1, Eaglets are fed raw meat. Eagles do not regurgitate food to feed their young like some other animals do. Eaglets are fed 1 to 8 times a day. The parents carry prey to the nest to feed their young. They feed the Eaglets by tearing off pieces of food and holding them to the beaks of their young.

Looking after baby

After 5 to 6 weeks, the parents are not in the nest full time, but at least 1 parent is always perching in the trees nearby.

Young Eaglets have the fastest growth rate of any North American bird. By the time they are 9 weeks old, the Eaglets are fully grown.

Brown eyes
Dark head feathers
Dark beak
Dark tail feathers
A Juvenile Bald Eagle

By 8 weeks, the Eaglets are strong enough to flap their wings, lift their feet off the nest, and rise up in the air. Eaglets start to fly from 10 to 14 weeks of age, though they still remain close to the nest. Even after they first learn to fly, their parents still look after the young Eaglets for another 6 weeks.

About 8 weeks after their first flight Eaglets start to leave the nest and their parents. They are now between 3.5 and 5 months old.

More Cool Bald Eagle Facts:

1. It has been estimated that the gripping power (pounds per square inch) of the Bald Eagle is 10 times more than that of a human.

2. Bald Eagles in flight can be identified by their wings. If the wings are almost flat, it may be a Bald Eagle. Otherwise, it may be a Vulture or a Hawk.

3. As many as 4,000 Bald Eagles can gather on a riverbank during Salmon spawning season.

4. When a Bald Eagle loses a feather on one wing, it will lose a feather on the other wing in order to remain perfectly balanced.

5. Eagles (of different species) are the National Bird of Austria, Germany, Kazakhstan, Mexico and the USA.

6. The beak, talons, and feathers are made of keratin - the same stuff your finger and toe nails are made of.

7. American Eagle Day is celebrated annually on June 20. This day commemorates the day when the Bald Eagle was added to the Seal of the USA in 1782. First commemorated in 1995, it is now officially recognized in 41 different US states.

Do Bald Eagles Migrate?

In most of the areas that Bald Eagles call home, the Winters are really cold. What do Bald Eagles do in the Winter time? Do they migrate South like other birds?

It all depends on where home is and where they breed.

Bald Eagles that breed in areas that don't get that cold in the Winter stay exactly where they are.

Bald Eagles that breed in areas where it freezes and is very cold do migrate. Bald Eagles that breed in cold areas inland will migrate to warmer areas along the coast for Winter. Other Bald Eagles that breed in the North migrate to warmer areas in the South for Winter.

Bald Eagles do not migrate in flocks, like other birds. They migrate alone or with their breeding partner.

How and Where do Bald Eagles Sleep?

Bald Eagles sleep just like us humans do. They go to sleep after the Sun sets and sleep during the night. They wake up as soon as the Sun comes up.

Bald Eagles have a specialized mechanism in each foot that allows them to lock it in position so they can sleep without falling out of a tree. This is similar to a horse sleeping standing up.

When they are incubating eggs, one adult will spend the night on the eggs in the nest. Adults will spend time in the nest when their Eaglets are very young.

At other times, adult Bald Eagles sleep on a branch of a tree.

Aerial Acrobats

Mates, or courting pairs, lock their talons together.

They spin and cartwheel through the air, and only let go of one another just before they hit the ground.

Male and female locking talons

How have Bald Eagles Adapted to their Environment?

Excellent hearing

Fantastic eyesight to see prey

Strong curved beak to rip into prey

Protective head feathers

Long, broad wings for gliding

Dark body feathers absorb sunlight, keeps the bird warm

Strong wide tail for balance in flight

Powerful talons to grab and carry prey

THREATS

Even though Bald Eagles are no longer an endangered species, they still need our protection.

Bald Eagles still face many threats:

Predators

Adult Bald Eagles are at the top of the food chain, so they are not bothered by predators but eggs and Eaglets are at risk. Squirrels, Raccoons, Ravens, Crows and the great Horned Owl do attack eggs or Eaglets on the rare occasion when the parents leave the nest unattended.

Lead Poisoning

Bald Eagles eat carrion that have been shot by humans using lead bullets. By eating the flesh which contains lead, Bald Eagles can die of lead poisoning. Millions of birds are affected by lead poisoning other than Bald Eagles. Lead poisoning is one of the main causes of Bald Eagle deaths.

Chemical Pollutants

Even though pesticides like DDT have been banned in the USA, they are still used in Mexico. Cross border winds carries the DDT into the USA. Pesticides leach into the rivers, and fish absorb it into their bodies. Bald Eagles catching these fish are now eating these pesticides causing them harm, and even death.

Electrocution

Bald Eagles are electrocuted when they fly into power lines in poor visibility weather. Many are electrocuted when they sit on high voltage power lines and touch the power cable and the ground at the same time. Electrocution is a major source of Bald Eagle deaths.

Wind Turbines

As we use more sources of alternative energy, more and more wind farms are being built. Millions of birds and bats are being killed every year by flying into the blades of wind turbines, and the number keeps growing as we build more wind farms. Bald Eagles are one bird species that are being killed by wind turbines.

Habitat Destruction

As the human population grows, we are taking away more and more of the Bald Eagle's natural habitat. Humans are building more properties along coastal areas and river fronts - the places that Bald Eagles like to live and catch their food. Although there are protected areas where no buildings can be built - Bald Eagles cover a much greater area than these protected areas.

Poaching

Many Bald Eagles are still being illegally hunted by poachers for their feathers, or by farmers that fear that Bald Eagles are preying on their livestock.

THANKS FOR READING!

Please leave a review at your favorite bookseller's website.
Share with other readers what you liked about this book.

Visit www.TJRob.com to learn about other exciting books by TJ Rob:

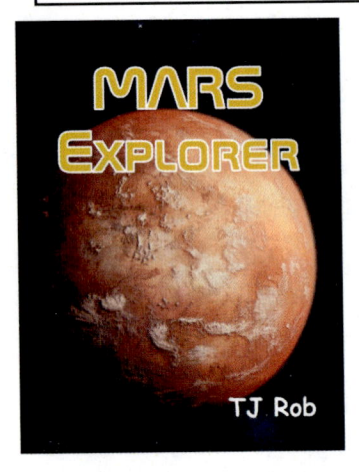

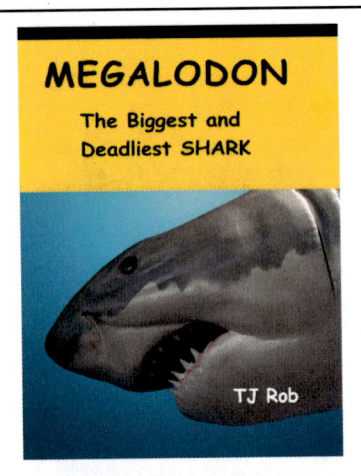

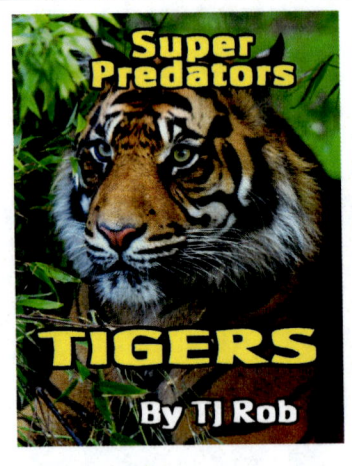

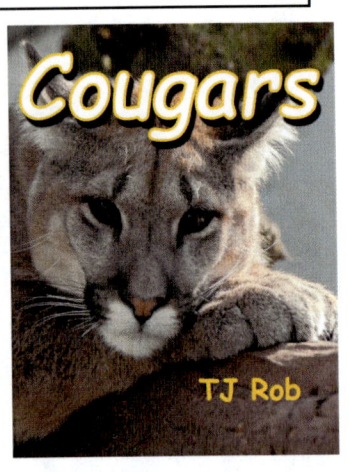

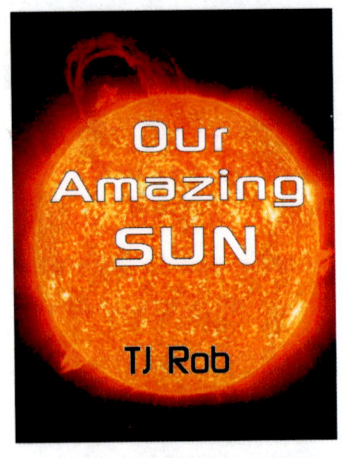

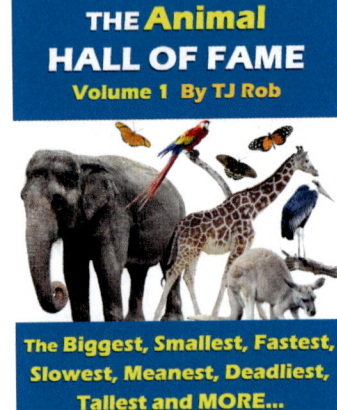

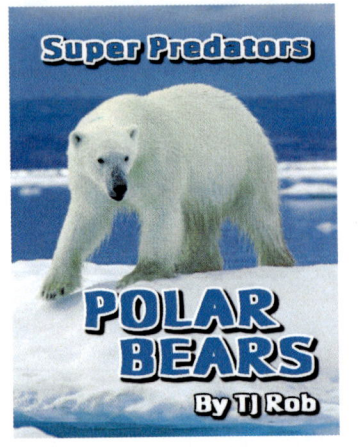

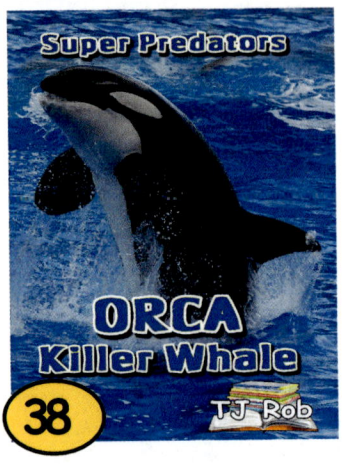

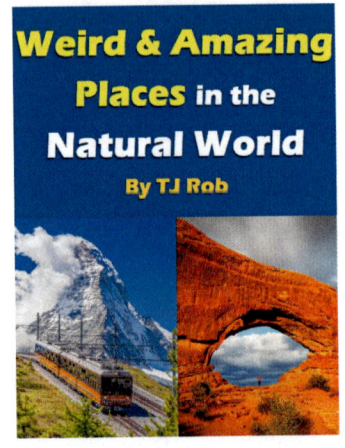

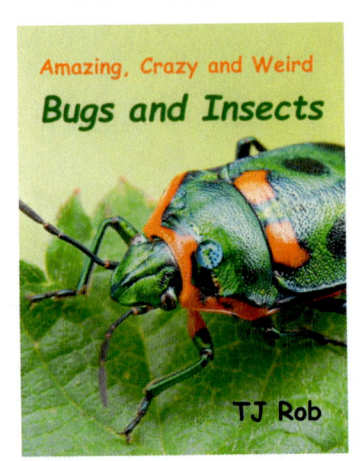

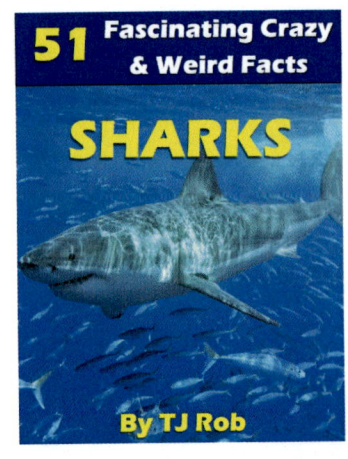

Made in the USA
Las Vegas, NV
26 November 2022